Before reading this book, the

- two or more letters can repre
- the spelling <oi> can represent the sound 'oi '

This book introduces:
- the spelling <oi> for the sound 'oi '
- text at 2 syllable level

High-frequency words:
the, oh, no, says, I, book, she, to, two, so, Mr, have, you, me, I'd, love

Vocabulary:
soil   – loose earth that plants grow in
coins   – pieces of metal money
join me   – come with me

Talk about the story

Nan can't drive her fab cab. Black oil is dripping from it. What should Nan do? How will she fix it?

Reading Practice

Practise blending these sounds into words:

oi l

b oi l

c oi n

j oi n

s oi l

p oi nt

sp oi l

t oi let

Oil

Drip! Drip! Oil drips from the fab cab. "Oh no!" says Nan. "I must fix the dripping oil!"

"I can fix the fab cab," says Nan.

Nan gets the spell book.

She points to the spell in the book.

Nan gets oil and soil and mixes them up. She adds two coins. "This will fix the fab cab!"

Nan points at the fab cab. ZAP!

"Oink, oink!" says the pig. "This is bad!" says Nan.

So Nan gets Mr Toil to help.

"I have spoilt the cab!" says Nan.

Mr Toil fixes the dripping oil.

"Mr Toil, will you join me in the fab cab?" Nan asks. "I'd love to join you!" says Mr Toil.

Questions for discussion:

- What is wrong with Nan's car?

- How does she try to fix it?

- Where do you think she will take Mr Toil in her car?

Game with <oi> words

Play as pelmanism or use for reading practice. Enlarge and photocopy the page twice on two different colours of card. Cut the cards up to play.
Ensure the players sound out the words.

oil	soil	boil
point	coin	foil
hoist	join	moist
spoil	toil	avoid